Expressions
of Women in
Ministry

Dana Easterling

Expressions of Women in Ministry

Copyright 2021 Dana Easterling ISBN: 9780-0-578-35494-1
Request for information should be emailed to Dana Easterling:
2danaeast@gmail.com

Bible Translations and permissions:
Scripture quotations marked (NIV) are taken from the Holy Bible, New International Version®, NIV®. Copyright © 1973, 1978, 1984, 2011 by Biblica, Inc.™ Used by permission of Zondervan. All rights reserved worldwide. www.zondervan.com. The "NIV" and "New International Version" are trademarks registered in the United States Patent and Trademark Office by Biblica, Inc.™ "Scripture quotations taken from the (NASB®) New American Standard Bible®, Copyright © 1960, 1971, 1977, 1995, 2020 by The Lockman Foundation. Used by permission. All rights reserved. www.lockman.org" [Scripture quotations are from] Common Bible: New Revised Standard Version Bible, copyright © 1989 National Council of the Churches of Christ in the United States of America. Used by permission. All rights reserved worldwide. Scripture quotations marked TPT are from The Passion Translation®. Copyright © 2017, 2018 by Passion & Fire Ministries, Inc. Used by permission. All rights reserved. ThePassionTranslation.com. Scripture quotations marked (AMP) are taken from the Amplified Bible, Copyright © 2015 by The Lockman Foundation. Used by permission. www.lockman.org"Scripture quotations are from the ESV® Bible (The Holy Bible, English Standard Version®), copyright © 2001 by Crossway, a publishing ministry of Good News Publishers. Used by permission. All rights reserved." The Strong's Exhaustive Concordance of the Bible by James Strong (1890) is public domain

Cover design: Cheryl Easterling

Foreword

Dana is a man of God that I have come to know and respect. His love for God and his desire to see women set free to minister as God designed is beautiful to behold. The devoted way in which Dana has searched the scriptures to find the heart of our Loving Abba Father's regarding women in ministry powerfully expresses his Shepherd's heart for both men and women in the body of Christ. As a follower of Christ for over 50 years, I have had the privilege of serving as both a pastor and missionary; I have been blessed to see women of God walking in their unique anointing in many places around the world. As women follow their calling faithfully seeking the leading of the Holy Spirit, hearts and lives are changed for the better. In these times it is more important than ever for believers to understand how God views women. This book will help you look at this issue from God's point of view. I encourage you to read Dana's book with an open spirit as you look to see all that God planned for women when He created us. The possibilities are simply amazing! As you read this book, please pray for God to allow you to see how He wants you to fulfill your unique calling in the Kingdom. Most importantly, don't be afraid to dream big! We serve an awesome God who is not only here to make you feel secure - He designed for you to be a powerful part of His plan! Men of God, I pray that you are able to support the women of God in your life to fully walk in their God-given anointing. I know that you will be blessed as you do! Women of God, it's time to rise up with wings as eagles, it's time to spread your wings and fly!

Julianne Kobelin M.A.

Preface

Let me begin by sharing a little of my story.

I trusted Jesus as savior about 35 years ago. My wife had trusted Jesus 3 years before me, and at that time we were part of a mainline denominational church. Immediately after trusting Christ I began devouring God's written word. I remember reading the New Testament several times in the first two weeks as a Christian. My wife and I also promptly began serving in the church, and in a short time we were the youth leaders. A couple of years after that I was ordained as a deacon in the church. I had been reading and studying the Bible a lot for a few years at this point and had been noticing things written in the Bible that we did not do in our church, and also many of the same things were openly spoken against, either in our group gatherings or in private conversations. I remember having a conversation with my pastor about these things and his response was that the things in the Bible to which I was referring to were no longer part of the Christian experience. I promptly said "Where does it say that in the Bible?" To which he responded, "It doesn't say that in the Bible."

I am very grateful for that moment in my life, as I know it was a "God Moment," for me. In that moment a line was drawn in the sand for me. Did I really believe God's written word or did I believe a man who was teaching, saying, and doing things clearly contrary to God's perfect written word? I am so grateful for my first pastor challenging me on the scriptures as it caused me to take a stand on God's written word. That experience instilled a habit in me that has never diminished. To read, study, pray, and meditate on the scriptures and whatever the scriptures are clear on believe it and do it. This attitude toward the Bible mixed with an intimate relationship with Jesus has produced a precious closeness with God, and a wonderfully satisfying life!

My wife and I have served together in ministry for over 30 years. From the beginning we had other men either through their preaching, teaching or actions highlight the differences between the male and female genders in regard to what positions each gender could occupy and function in Christ's church.

They would point out the scriptures that Paul wrote to support their position. For many years my wife and I served together. For most of those years we co-led various ministries as it was clear to me and others that both her and I were called and anointed to do what we were doing. Seeing the call on my wife and other women's lives created somewhat of a struggle in me. I knew these women were clearly called, anointed and empowered to be leaders in Christ's Church. So for many years I prayed about this and referred to the few scriptures that Paul wrote restricting women; While, at the same time, seeing God use my wife and other women in mighty ways. Another thing was also happening during those contemplative years. I began seeing women in leadership spoken of in many places in the Bible. Holy Spirit was leading me into the whole truth regarding women in leadership. This book is the result of the God given revelation and resolution the scriptures gave me.

I pray this book will be helpful to you as you follow Jesus. Now let's get to it!

Dana Easterling

Contents

Introduction

The purpose of this book is to present a Biblical perspective on women in ministry. It is my belief that this is such an important issue that it absolutely requires extensive Biblical research, and with that research, produce a document in writing for all to see.

My approach in gathering the information in this book was to look at the many scriptural examples that speak of women in both the Old and New Testaments, with the ultimate goal being to uncover God's heart on this issue through the preponderance of scriptures and Biblical evidence. I also considered a limited amount of historically relevant information, as there were significant cultural, religious, and social issues of that time that were being addressed through some of the scriptures regarding women. Finally, after sharing the Biblical pattern of women in ministry, I explored the continuation of that pattern as it carries on to the present day.

The Bible, cover to cover, is our perfect guidebook for us individually and Jesus' Church collectively. It teaches that leaders and teachers will receive a stricter judgment (James 3:1). Since I myself and other leaders and teachers will be held accountable to a higher standard, we must do just as Paul instructed Timothy:

Study and do your best to present yourself to God approved, a workman [tested by trial] who has no reason to be ashamed, accurately handling and skillfully teaching the word of truth.
2 Timothy 2:15 (AMP)

Let's begin on the foundation that:

16 Every Scripture has been written by the Holy Spirit, the breath of God. It will empower you by its instruction and correction, giving you the strength to take the right direction and lead you deeper into the path of godliness. 17 Then you will be God's servant, fully mature and perfectly prepared to fulfill any assignment God gives you. 2 Timothy 3:16-17 (TPT)

With the scriptures as our guide, now let's look at the many verses regarding women.

Expressions of Women in Ministry

Old Testament Expressions of Women in Ministry

In Genesis we see man and woman before sin enters humanity and God curses mankind. This pre-curse state gives us a great starting point to begin our journey through this subject, as this pre-curse condition reveals to us God's original design for man and women. It is also important to note that when someone trusts Christ as savior they are restored to this pre-curse/original design state.

Expressions of Women in Ministry

Then God said, "Let Us make man in Our image, according to Our likeness; and let them rule over the fish of the sea and over the birds of the sky and over the cattle and over all the earth, and over every creeping thing that creeps on the earth."
Genesis 1:26 (NASB)

God the Father, God the Son and God the Holy Spirit decided to make man and women in their image and likeness.

So God created mankind in his own image, in the image of God he created them; male and female he created them. Genesis 1:27 (NIV)

God the Father, God the Son, and God the Holy Spirit each have unique personalities and unique characteristics yet all three live and exist in absolute unity. In this verse we see that God created them male and female with His characteristics.

The 3 persons who are our God shared His male characteristics with the man and His female characteristics with the woman.

We also see in Genesis 1:26 that God created male and female to be like God, the three totally unified persons who are our one God; created male and female human beings to live, move and have their beings in unity.

God created the man Adam first and:

Then the Lord God said, "It is not good for the man to be alone; I will make him a helper suitable for him." Genesis 2:18 (NASB)

The Strong's concordance interprets it this way: I will make him a helper opposite to him, i.e. a counterpart, an equal opposite to himself. A helper that is in front of, in sight of, opposite to. Also meaning: to stand opposite someone to speak by word of mouth to them.

So, a helper suitable means: an opposite, equal helper of man.

This scripture teaches us that Eve was Adam's "Opposite, equal other half." Equal to him, but infused by God with opposite qualities. This means that God did not create woman to be inferior to man, nor did God create man to be superior to woman. God created both genders as equal opposites.

Then:

God blessed them; and God said to them, "Be fruitful and multiply, and fill the earth, and subdue it; and rule over the fish of the sea and over the birds of the sky and over every living thing that moves on the earth." Genesis 1:28 (NASB)

In this verse and also in Genesis 1:26 God gave both the man and the woman dominion over all of the earth to rule and reign.

Verse 28 also says that men and women are to:
Be fruitful-We are to have lives that are very fruitful and productive.

Multiply- To have children and increase our family's size. Fill the earth with male and female children and together both genders are to have dominion over His creation.

In Genesis chapter 3 verse 6 Adam and Eve sin against God. In verse 6, when they both disobey God, even in that act there was shared leadership, as there is no evidence that Adam questioned Eve as she handed him the fruit to eat. Adam fully trusted Eve's leadership and without question ate the fruit she handed him.

6 When the woman saw that the fruit of the tree was good for food and pleasing to the eye, and also desirable for gaining wisdom, she took some and ate it. She also gave some to her husband, who was with her, and he ate it. Genesis 3:6 (NIV)

According to the Bible Adam followed Eve's lead in this instance. Then the Lord God questions them as to whether they had eaten from the tree or not.

12 The man said, "The woman whom You gave to be with me, she gave me from the tree, and I ate." 13 Then the Lord God said to the woman, "What is this you have done?" And the woman said, "The serpent deceived me, and I ate." Genesis 3:12-13 (NASB)

Expressions of Women in Ministry

In the previous two verses in Genesis we see Adam respond to the Lord, and in his answer we see shared authority as Eve took the initiative and gave Adam the fruit to eat. After they committed the sin, God curses both the man and woman. The curse upon Eve (affecting all of womankind) is:

To the woman he said, "I will make your pains in childbearing very severe; with painful labor you will give birth to children. Your desire will be for your husband, and he will rule over you."
Genesis 3:16 (NIV)

Before Adam and Eve sinned they ruled and reigned as equals, partners in everything. But, after the curse, their relational dynamic radically changed. Man and woman went from sharing authority and responsibility, co-ruling and reigning on the earth, to a complete position change of man ruling woman.

There is another important aspect of the curse upon womankind that solidified the position change of man ruling woman. It is the part of the curse that created a strong longing and desire in woman for man. This strong desire for man mixed with a woman's gentler, caring and nurturing qualities created the perfect relational dynamic for the curse to dominate the lives of man and womankind.

The curse upon the serpent (Satan) also reinforces womankind's post curse subservient position. We see this in Genesis 3:15

And I will put enmity between you and the woman, and between your offspring and hers; he will crush your head, and you will strike his heel." Genesis 3:15 (NIV)

God said I will put enmity (personal hostility), between you and the woman. Satan exists in a state of personal hostility against womankind. This curse upon the serpent was also a prophecy of the coming Messiah Jesus, who was born through woman and crushed his head. Satan does everything in his power to keep women in that cursed, subservient position.

In the previous verses in Genesis we saw man and womankind in their pre-curse, original design state where they enjoyed unrestricted fellowship with God. They also ruled and reigned as uniquely different equals as well. The curses God pronounced upon them after they disobeyed Him radically changed everything for all of humanity. That is, until Jesus. Who through His perfect life, sacrifice and resurrection, provided the way for all who trust in Him to be restored back to that pre-curse state, fully restoring unbroken fellowship with God. This was indicated by the torn veil of the temple after Jesus death (Matthew 27:51). Also, there is now no condemnation to those of us who are in Christ; no separation, no more living under the curse. Romans 8:1 Praise God!

Therefore, there is now no condemnation for those who are in Christ Jesus. Romans 8:1 (NIV)

Old Testament Examples of Women Leaders

The Old Testament scriptures reveal a male-dominated society. However, as we shall see there are many examples of women serving God in various leadership positions.

Sarah A wise councilor to Abraham; Listed in the Hebrews chapter 11 "Hall of faith"

God said to Abraham, "Do not let it distress you because of Ishmael and your maid; whatever Sarah tells you, listen to her and do what she asks, for your

descendants will be named through Isaac.
Genesis 21:12 (AMP)

Miriam A prophetess and leader

In Micah 6:4 the prophet Micah identifies Miriam as one of the three leaders sent by God to bring Israel out of Egypt.

"For I brought you up from the land of Egypt And ransomed you from the house of slavery, And I sent before you Moses [to lead you], Aaron [the high priest], and Miriam [the prophetess].
Micah 6:4 (AMP)

As we see in Micah 6:4 God sent Moses, Aaron, and Miriam before the people. These three were God's chosen leaders of the Israelites at this time. And Moses refers to Miriam as a prophetess in Exodus:

Then Miriam the prophetess, the sister of Aaron [and Moses], took a timbrel in her hand, and all the women followed her with timbrels and dancing.
Exodus 15:20 (AMP)

Deborah A judge, prophetess, and leader in Israel. Serving as a judge was the highest leadership position in Israel at that time.

4 Now Deborah, a prophetess, the wife of Lappidoth, was judging Israel at that time. 5 She used to sit [to hear and decide disputes] under the palm tree of Deborah between Ramah and Bethel in the hill country of Ephraim; and the Israelites came up to her for judgment. Judges 4:4-5 (AMP)

6 Now she sent word and summoned Barak the son of Abinoam from Kedesh-naphtali, and said to him, "Behold, the Lord, the God of Israel, has commanded, 'Go and march to Mount Tabor, and take with you ten thousand men [of war] from the tribes of Naphtali and Zebulun. 7 I will draw out Sisera, the commander of Jabin's army, with his chariots and his infantry to meet you at the river Kishon, and I will hand him over to you.'" 8 Then Barak said to her, "If you will go with

me, then I will go; but if you will not go with me, I will not go." 9 She said, "I will certainly go with you;

nevertheless, the journey that you are about to take will not be for your honor and glory, because the Lord will sell Sisera into the hand of a woman." Then Deborah got up and went with Barak to Kedesh. Judges 4:6-9 (AMP)

Villagers in Israel would not fight; they held back until I, Deborah, arose, until I arose, a mother in Israel. Judges 5:7 (NIV)

We see in these verses that Deborah was a judge, prophetess, and leader that had tremendous influence. And because of the Lord's leadership grace upon Deborah's life, the Bible says at the end of Judges chapter 5 in verse 31:

Then the land had peace forty years. Judges 5:31(NIV)

Hannah A prophetess who prophesied of the coming messiah in 1 Samuel 2:10

Isaiah's wife A prophetess

Then I made love to the prophetess, and she conceived

and gave birth to a son. And the Lord said to me,
"Name him Maher-Shalal-Hash-Baz. Isaiah 8:3 (NIV)

Huldah- A prophet & teacher that changed the course
of Israel

In 2 Kings 22 In the eighteenth year of King Josiah's
reign, Hilkiah the high priest finds a copy of the Torah
that had been hidden and he gives it to Shaphan the
secretary. Shaphan takes the scroll to the king and
reads it in his presence.

Now when the king heard the words of the Book of the
Law, he tore his clothes. 2 Kings 22:11(AMP)

Then the king sends a group of his most trusted
officials including the priest and the scribe, telling
them to:

"Go, inquire of the Lord for my sake and for the sake
of the people and for all Judah concerning the words
of this book which has been found.
2 Kings 22:13 (AMP)

So Hilkiah and those whom the king had sent went to the prophet Huldah and she prophesies the word of the Lord to the messengers to convey to the king. Which they do, and then King Josiah responds to the Lord wholeheartedly. *2 Chronicles 34:22a (NRSV)*

Here we see the king of Israel sending his most trusted officials to the prophet Huldah so that she can authenticate the document and also prophesy a message from God to the king. When the king hears the prophecy from Huldah he responds wholeheartedly.

Note: The prophets Jeremiah and Zephaniah were also alive at that time but, the King chose to trust Huldah with this extremely important matter.

Esther Author of the book of Esther, queen, and a woman hero who saves the Jewish people.

Women Who served at the entrance to the tent of meeting (1 Samuel 2:22).

David Speaks of Women of War

in Psalm 68:11-12

11 God Almighty declares the word of the gospel with power, and the warring women of Zion deliver its message: 12 "The conquering legions have themselves been conquered. Look at them flee!" Now Zion's women are left to gather the spoils.
Psalm 68:11-12 (TPT)

These many examples of women leaders in the Old Testament provide a pattern of God's leadership grace upon women's lives, as these women leaders were clearly called, empowered, and anointed to function in their leadership positions.

New Testament Expressions of Women in Ministry

Now we will look at the New Testament. And just as with the Old Testament these scriptures were written in a male-dominated society. However, as we saw many scriptural examples of women leaders in the Old Testament, we will see the Biblical pattern continue with many more examples of women leaders in the New Testament.

In John 4:1-42 Jesus speaks with a woman at a well and she believes in Him. When the disciples return, they are stunned to see Jesus speaking with the Samaritan woman. This Samaritan woman then goes back into her village and talks with them about Jesus telling them to come out and meet a man who could be the messiah. The townspeople responded to her evangelism/preaching and came out to the well where they met Jesus personally and their lives were changed. Jesus chose to appear to women first after He was resurrected and He instructed them to relay His orders to the men (Matthew 28:1-10). These women were the first "Sent ones" after His resurrection.

Matthew 28:1-10 Now after the Sabbath, near dawn of the first day of the week, Mary Magdalene and the other Mary went to look at the tomb. 2 And a great earthquake had occurred, for an angel of the Lord descended from heaven and came and rolled away the stone [from the opening of the tomb], and sat on it. 3 The angel's appearance was like lightning, and his clothes were as white as snow. 4 The guards shook, paralyzed with fear [at the sight] of him and became like dead men [pale and immobile]. 5 But the angel said to the women, "Do not be afraid; for I know that you are looking for Jesus who has been crucified. 6 He is not here, for He has risen, just as He said [He would]. Come! See the place where He was lying. 7 Then go quickly and tell His disciples that He has risen from the dead; and behold, He is going ahead of you into Galilee [as He promised]. There you will see Him; behold, I have told you." 8 So the women left the [the good news to] the disciples. 9 And as they went, suddenly, Jesus met them, saying, "Rejoice!" And they went to Him and took hold of His feet [in homage] and worshiped Him [as the Messiah]. 10 Then Jesus said to them, "Do not be afraid; go and tell My brothers to leave for Galilee, and there they will see Me [just as I promised]." Matthew 28:1-10 (AMP)

Expressions of Women in Ministry

New Testament Women in Leadership and Other Scriptures Regarding Women

In Acts chapter 2 on the day of Pentecost when the disciples were baptized in the Holy Spirit, Peter preaches:

Acts 2:17-18 (NIV) "'In the last days, God says, I will pour out my Spirit on all people. Your sons and daughters will prophesy, your young men will see visions, your old men will dream dreams. 18 Even on

my servants, both men and women, I will pour out my
Spirit in those days, and they will prophesy.

Peter was quoting Joel 2:28-32.

Let's read what Saul (Paul) did to believers in
Acts 8:3(TPT)

Then Saul mercilessly persecuted the church of God,
going from house to house into the homes of believers
to arrest both men and women and drag them off to
prison. Acts 8:3 (TPT)

The fact that Saul went from house to house arresting
both men and women means that both genders were
sharing the gospel with others.

Philip the evangelist had four daughters that were
prophetesses.

8 On the next day we left and came to Caesarea, and
entering the house of Philip the evangelist, who was
one of the seven, we stayed with him. 9 Now this man
had four virgin daughters who were prophetesses.
Acts 21:8-9 (NASB)

Paul list 2 women and one man in Philippians 4:2-3 who had "Labored at his side in the cause of the gospel."

2 And I plead with Euodia and Syntyche to settle their disagreement and be restored with one mind in our Lord. 3 I would like my dear friend and burden-bearer to help resolve this issue, for both women have diligently labored with me for the prize and helped in spreading the revelation of the gospel, along with Clement and the rest of my coworkers. All of their names are written in the Book of Life.
Philippians 4:2-3 (TPT)

And in Romans chapter 16 Paul says:

6 Greet Mary, who worked very hard for you. 12 Greet Tryphena and Tryphosa, those women who work hard in the Lord. Greet my beloved Persis, who has worked hard in the Lord. Romans 16:6&12 (NIV)

In these verses Paul states that these women had labored or worked hard in the ministry. The Greek word used here is (kopiáō), used many other times for the labor of ministry. See also (1 Corinthians 16:16; 1 Thessalonians 5:12; 1 Timothy 5:17).

Anna A Prophet/Preacher

36 There was also a prophet, Anna the daughter of Phanuel, of the tribe of Asher. She was of a great age, having lived with her husband seven years after her marriage, 37 then as a widow to the age of eighty-four. She never left the temple but worshiped there with fasting and prayer night and day. 38 At that moment she came, and began to praise God and to speak about the child to all who were looking for the redemption of Jerusalem. *Luke 2:36-38(NRSV)*

Phoebe A deacon, leader, letter carrier, and helper of Paul and others. Phoebe is not mentioned alongside a husband, so it is probable that she was a single lady or a widow. Phoebe was a deacon in the church at Cenchreae. She was also a leader/letter carrier/and helper of Paul.

1 I commend to you our sister Phoebe, a deacon of the church at Cenchreae, 2 so that you may welcome her

in the Lord as is fitting for the saints, and help her in
whatever she may require from you, for she has been a
benefactor of many and of myself as well.
Romans 16:1-2 (NRSV)

In Romans 16:1 Paul commends to the church at
Rome sister Phoebe who is a deacon of the church in
Cenchrea. Deacon is the Greek word diakonos. Paul
uses this same word in other verses for ministers and
leaders in Christ church.

In Romans 16:2 The Greek term translated *benefactor*
here is prostatis, which indicates that this female
deacon also had an impressive Christian reputation and
that she cared for the affairs of others and also helped
them with her resources.

Also of note is the way Paul instructs the church to
help this female leader in *whatever* she needs. This
statement by Paul farther speaks to her trusted
leadership.

Based on these two verses in Romans, we see that Paul
knew and trusted Phoebe, trusting her so much that he

chose her to personally deliver his letter to the Romans.

As we saw in the previous 2 verses, Phoebe was a trusted leader in the church.

Priscilla A pastor/minister/ teacher/ leader

Priscilla and Aquila were a wife and husband team that ministered together.

Romans 16:3-5a (ESV) 3 Greet Prisca and Aquila, my fellow workers in Christ Jesus, 4 who risked their necks for my life, to whom not only I give thanks but all the churches of the Gentiles give thanks as well. 5 Greet also the church in their house.

This husband and wife were fellow workers of Paul.

Priscilla the "**fellow worker**" in the Lord; this is the same word that Paul uses in the following references.

Timothy-

*Romans 16:21 (AMP) Timothy, my **fellow worker**,*

sends his greetings to you, as do Lucius, Jason and Sosipater, my kinsmen.

Titus-

*2 Corinthians 8:23 (AMP) As for Titus, he is my partner and **fellow worker** in your service; and as for the [other two] brothers, they are [special] messengers of the churches, a glory and credit to Christ.*

Philemon-

*Philemon 1:1 (AMP) Paul, a prisoner [for the sake] of Christ Jesus (the Messiah, the Anointed), and our brother Timothy, To Philemon our dearly beloved friend and **fellow worker**,*

Mark, Aristarchus, Demas, and Luke-

*Philemon 1:24 (AMP) and from Mark, Aristarchus, Demas, and Luke, my **fellow workers**.*

And others; see also:

*Romans 16:9 (AMP) Greet Urbanus, our **fellow worker** in Christ, and my beloved Stachys*

Expressions of Women in Ministry

*Philippians 2:25 (ESV) I have thought it necessary to send to you Epaphroditus my brother and **fellow worker** and fellow soldier, and your messenger and minister to my need,*

*Colossians 4:11 (ESV) and Jesus who is called Justus. These are the only men of the circumcision among my **fellow workers** for the kingdom of God, and they have been a comfort to me.*

In the verses in Romans we just looked at, Paul refers to Priscilla and Aquila and the church that meets in their house. In the Scriptures Priscilla and Aquila are mentioned together, which tells us that this wife and husband worked and ministered together as a team.

In Ephesus a Jew named Apollos spoke to the people about the Lord. He taught about Jesus accurately, though he only knew of the baptism of John.

Acts 18:26(NIV) He began to speak boldly in the synagogue. When Priscilla and Aquila heard him, they invited him to their home and explained to him the way of God more adequately.

Both Priscilla and Aquila took Apollos aside and taught him. In the Bible Paul and Luke wrote Priscilla's name first when speaking of this wife and husband. In light of the fact that the scriptures speaking of this wife and husband were written in a male dominated society, Paul and Luke were clearly *going against the grain* in doing this, which highlights the leadership of Priscilla.

See also:

Acts 18:18 (NIV) Paul stayed on in Corinth for some time. Then he left the brothers and sisters and sailed for Syria, accompanied by Priscilla and Aquila.

2 Timothy 4:19 (NIV) Greet Priscilla and Aquila and the household of Onesiphorus.

According to the Bible Priscilla functioned as a pastor/teacher/minister and leader in the early church alongside her husband.

Junia A woman Apostle

In Romans 16 verse 7 Paul sends greetings to

Expressions of Women in Ministry

Andronicus and Junia who are outstanding among the apostles.

Following are 2 different Bible translations of this verse:

7 Greet Andronicus and Junia, my relatives who were in prison with me; they are prominent among the apostles, and they were in Christ before I was. Romans 16:7(NRSV)

7 Make sure that my relatives Andronicus and Junia are honored, for they're my fellow captives who bear the distinctive mark of being outstanding and well-known apostles, and who were joined into the Anointed One before me. Romans 16:7 (TPT)

Junia is a feminine name, and as we just saw in the previous scripture, Paul recognizes Junia as an apostle. The early church father, John Chrysostom (c. AD 349 – 407), commenting on this verse, said,

"'Greet Andronicus and Junia .distinguished among the apostles.' To be apostles is a great thing, but to be distinguished among them—consider what an extraordinary accolade that is! They were distinguished because of their works and because of their upright deeds. Indeed, how great was the wisdom of this woman that she was thought worthy of being called an apostle!"

Some scriptures that speak of qualities, roles and responsibilities of an Apostle are:

The things that distinguish a true apostle were performed among you with great perseverance—supernatural signs, startling wonders, and awesome miracles. 2 Corinthians 12:12 (TPT)

And God has placed in the church first of all apostles, second prophets, third teachers, then miracles, then gifts of healing, of helping, of guidance, and of different kinds of tongues. 1 Corinthians 12:28 (NIV)

11 So Christ himself gave the apostles, the prophets, the evangelists, the pastors and teachers, 12 to equip his people for works of service, so that the body of Christ may be built up 13 until we all reach unity in the faith and in the knowledge of the Son of God and become mature, attaining to the whole measure of the fullness of Christ. Ephesians 4:11-13 (NIV)

For the Apostle Paul to refer to Junia as an outstanding Apostle is amazing! Junia had to have exhibited the required evidences necessary or Paul would not have called her an Apostle.

The position of Apostle is according to 1Corinthians 12:28, the position of greatest authority in Christ church.

1Corinthians 12:28(ESV) And God has appointed in the church first apostles, second prophets, third teachers, then miracles, then gifts of healing, helping, administrating, and various kinds of tongues.

Lydia   A leader/ successful business woman
In Acts 16:14-15 A business woman named Lydia believed in the Lord, and as seen in verse 15 she was the head of her home.

Acts 16:14-15(NIV) 14 One of those listening was a woman from the city of Thyatira named Lydia, a dealer in purple cloth. She was a worshiper of God. The Lord opened her heart to respond to Paul's message. 15 When she and the members of her household were baptized, she invited us to her home. "If you consider me a believer in the Lord," she said, "come and stay at my house." And she persuaded us.

Then in Acts 16:40 when Paul and Silas were released from prison they go to Lydia's house where they met with the believers.

Acts 16:40 (TPT) So Paul and Silas left the prison and went back to Lydia's house, where they met with the believers and comforted and encouraged them before departing.

Lydia was a leader in the community as well a woman of influence in the church in Philippi.

Nympha A church leader, pastor?
Nympha was a woman who had a church group that met in her house. The following verse does not

specifically say whether or not she was the pastor/shepherd of the church group that met in her home, but Paul is speaking to her in this verse as the leader/pastor of the church that gathered in her home.

Give my greetings to all the believers in Laodicea. And pray for dear Nymphas and the church that gathers in her home. Colossians 4:15 (TPT)

The letter of 2 John is addressed to a woman pastor/shepherd and the church group she led.

From the elder to God's chosen woman and her children: I love you all as those who are in the truth. And I'm not the only one, for all who come to know the truth share my love for you. 2 John 1 (TPT)

In the first verse of 2 John that we just read, we see John following the common practice of the day by stating who his letter is written to.

And the letter of 2 John closes with a greeting from another church group with its women pastor.

The children of your sister, whom God has chosen, send you their loving greetings. Amen.

2 John 13 (TPT)

Expressions of Women in Ministry

God's Heart on the Matter

These many examples of women serving God and His church in various leadership roles in the Bible should be seen as God's heart on the matter. Even if there were only a few examples of women with scripturally recognized leadership roles, that would be enough evidence to prove that God does call women to leadership positions in His church. And as we just saw there are not only a few, but many, many examples in both Old and New Testaments of women in leadership.

But wait. What about specific scriptures that restrict or exclude women from certain leadership positions and

expressions? We will look at some of those verses here. And in addition to looking at them, I will present a limited combination of Biblical and historical evidence in my attempt to better interpret Paul's meaning in the verses.

In John 2:1-11 Jesus was at a wedding with His mother Mary and they run out of wine. So, Mary informs Jesus that they are out of wine, implying by Jesus response that Mary had asked Him to perform a miracle and create some wine. Jesus does perform the miracle and make wine. This was Jesus first recorded miracle, which was initiated at Mary's leading.

John 2:1-11 (TPT) 1 Now on the third day, Jesus' mother went to a wedding feast in the Galilean village of Cana. 2–3 Jesus and his disciples were all invited to the banquet, but with so many guests, they ran out of wine. And when Mary realized it, she came to Jesus and asked, "They have no wine; can't you do something about it?" 4 Jesus replied, "My dear one, don't you understand that if I do this, it will change nothing for you, but it will change everything for me! My hour of unveiling my power has not yet come." 5 Mary then went to the servers and told them, "Whatever Jesus tells you, do it!" 6 Nearby stood six stone water pots meant to be used for the Jewish washing rituals. Each one could hold about twenty gallons or more. 7 Jesus came to the servers and instructed them, "Fill the pots with water, right up to the very brim." 8 Then he said, "Now fill your pitchers and take them to the master of ceremonies." 9 And when they poured out their pitchers for the master of ceremonies to sample, the water had become wine! When he tasted the water that had become wine, the master of ceremonies was impressed with its quality. (Although he didn't know where the wine had come from, only the servers knew.) He called the bridegroom over 10 and said to him, "Every host serves his best wine first, until everyone has had a cup or two, then he serves the cheaper wine. But you, my friend, you've reserved the most exquisite wine until now!" 11 This miracle in Cana was the first of the many extraordinary miracles Jesus performed in Galilee that revealed his glory, and his disciples believed in him.

This example in John of a woman (Mary) speaking up and exercising authority over a man (30 year old Jesus) telling Him what to do and Him doing it totally disagrees with two scriptures in 1 Timothy.

11 A woman must quietly receive instruction with entire submissiveness. 12 But I do not allow a woman to teach or exercise authority over a man, but to remain quiet.1 Timothy 2:11-12 (NASB)

Another similar scripture restricting women is:

The women should keep silent in the churches. For they are not permitted to speak, but should be in submission, as the Law also says.
1 Corinthians 14:34 (ESV)

However, just a few verses earlier in the same chapter Paul says in verse 31 that everyone may publically prophesy.

For you can all prophesy one by one, so that all may learn and all be encouraged,
1 Corinthians 14:31(ESV)

And in Chapter 11 verse 5 Paul says specifically that a woman can publically pray and prophesy.

And if any woman in a place of leadership within the church prays or prophesies in public with her long hair disheveled, she shows disrespect to her head, which is her husband, for this would be the same as having her head shaved. 1 Corinthians 11:5 (TPT)

We know historically that the church at Corinth was dealing with many problems and issues that Paul's letter was specifically addressing.

For a great article that sheds much light on the issues that the church at Corinth was dealing with, please read the article by Douglas A. Campbell at:

Expressions of Women in Ministry

https://www.christiancentury.org/article/critical-essay/paul-wrote-1-corinthians-community-middle-culture-war. I believe that the few scriptures Paul wrote greatly restricting or excluding women from certain expressions and positions of leadership were written by Paul as he was inspired by God to deal with specific problems and cultural issues.

There is significant historical evidence that supports this position. This document will only lightly touch on this historical fact. But, please look farther into the historical accounts of the issues that were affecting the early churches, particularly in Corinth and Ephesus on your own if you would like farther study on this.

In 1 Timothy chapter 3 and Titus 1:5-9 Paul states that an Overseer/Elder must be a man.

We will look at a portion of the scripture in 1Timothy

2 Yet an elder needs to be one who is without blame before others. He should be one whose heart is for his wife alone and not another woman. He should be recognized as one who is sensible, and well-behaved, and living a disciplined life. He should be a "spiritual shepherd" who has the gift of teaching, and is known for his hospitality. 1 Timothy 3:2 (TPT)

And Paul continues the list of qualifications and character qualities through verse 7 of 1Timothy chapter 3. There is also a similar list of requirements in Titus 1:5-9.

The scriptures in 1 Timothy and Titus have stringent requirements that must be met for anyone to serve in the official position of Elder/overseer/Pastor in the Church. When we read these verses, we must keep in mind the setting in which Paul and others were establishing the brand new Christian church.

Now let's look at some other verses that may shed some light on Paul's male only requirement in these verses.

In Acts chapter 16 Paul meets Timothy and wants Timothy to accompany himself and Silas on their missionary journey, but notice what Paul requires Timothy to do.

Expressions of Women in Ministry

Paul recognized God's favor on Timothy's life and wanted him to accompany them in ministry, but Paul had Timothy circumcised first because of the significant Jewish community living in the region, and everyone knew that Timothy's father wasn't a Jew. Acts 16:3 (TPT)

So we see that Paul had Timothy circumcised so the Jewish community would be more favorable towards Paul, Silas, Timothy and ultimately Jesus.

However circumcision is not a requirement for any Christian.

Look what Paul says in:

Galatians 5:2-3(TPT) 2 I, Paul, tell you: If you think there is benefit in circumcision and Jewish regulations, then you're acting as though Jesus the Anointed One is not enough. 3 I say it again emphatically: If you let yourselves be circumcised you are obliged to fulfill every single one of the commandments and regulations of the law!

And also in:

Galatians 5:6 (TPT) When you're joined to the Anointed One, circumcision and religious obligations can benefit you nothing.

And one more verse:

1 Corinthians 7:19a (TPT) Your identity before God has nothing to do with circumcision or uncircumcision.

We know that for the Jewish community, circumcision was a required part of being right with God.

We see how important this issue was in:

Acts 15:1 (TPT) 1 While Paul and Barnabas were in Antioch, some false teachers came from Judea to trouble the believers. They taught, "Unless you are circumcised, as the law of Moses requires, you cannot be saved."

These trouble makers were likely Pharisee converts that had trusted Christ, but still wanted to observe the law. They also expected every other Christian to be circumcised. Timothy's circumcision was to keep their group (and Christians in general) above reproach in the eyes of the Jewish communities that they visited.

The issue about circumcision was dealt with by the Church leaders at Jerusalem; their resolution on the issue was that no Christian needed to be circumcised.

Paul and the other early church leaders were doing their very best not to offend the Jewish community of their day. Now let's look at a few more verses in 1Timothy that speak of the requirements for Deacons. These verses pick up right after the Elder / Overseer / Pastor requirements which is what likewise is referring back to.

1 Timothy 3:8-10 & 12 (AMP) 8 Deacons likewise must be men worthy of respect [honorable, financially ethical, of good character], not double-tongued [speakers of half-truths], not addicted to wine, not greedy for dishonest gain, 9 but upholding and fully understanding the mystery [that is, the true doctrine] of the [Christian] faith with a clear conscience [resulting from behavior consistent with spiritual maturity]. 10 These men must first be tested; then if they are found to be blameless and beyond reproach [in their Christian lives], let them serve as deacons. 12 Deacons must be husbands of only one wife, and good managers of their children and their own households.

We see that according to these verses a Deacon must also be a man, but wait a minute; as we saw earlier in Romans 16 a woman named Phoebe was a Deacon.

Romans 16:1-2 (NRSV) 1 I commend to you our sister Phoebe, a deacon of the church at Cenchreae, 2 so that you may welcome her in the Lord as is fitting for the saints, and help her in whatever she may require from you, for she has been a benefactor of many and of myself as well.

None of us today fully understand why Paul wrote a few verses restricting women, and on the other hand the same Paul also wrote verses acknowledging and commending women leaders in the church.

It is as the Apostle Peter said of Paul:

16 He writes the same way in all his letters, speaking in them of these matters. His letters contain some things that are hard to understand.
2 Peter 3:16a (NIV)

If the Apostle Peter who walked with Jesus and was also an inspired writer of the Bible had a difficult time understanding what Paul meant in some scriptures, it should be no surprise that we would also have difficulty understanding some of what Paul wrote.

A few other verses that are significantly helpful in understanding the scriptures restricting women and also why Paul and other early church leaders required things of believers that are clearly not required of believers is:

1 Corinthians 9:19-23(TPT) 19 Now, even though I am free from obligations to others, I joyfully make myself a servant to all in order to win as many converts as possible. 20 I became Jewish to the Jewish people in order to win them to the Messiah. I became like one under the law to gain the people who were stuck under the law, even though I myself am not under the law. 21 And to those who are without the Jewish laws, I became like them, as one without the Jewish laws, in order to win them, although I'm not outside the law of God but under the law of Christ. 22 I became "weak" to the weak to win the weak. I have adapted to the culture of every place I've gone so that I could more easily win people to Christ. 23 I've done all this so that I would become God's partner for the sake of the gospel.

Paul was walking out *being all things to all people* so that he could win as many as possible to Christ. Paul did everything he could to establish Jesus Church in the midst of the culture, influences and problems of his day. He did a great job too! The verses we just looked at in 1 Corinthians 9 are extremely helpful in understanding why Paul wrote some verses restricting women and the same Paul also wrote many other verses recognizing women leaders. I believe that these verses help *connect the dots* so to speak as to why the same Apostle could write restrictive scriptures to women and also write scriptures acknowledging and commending women leaders.

Paul and other church leaders were wholeheartedly representing Jesus and trying to establish His church in the male dominated Jewish culture of their day. We have scriptural evidence that Paul and other early church leaders required things of Christians that God did not require of them. These leaders were wisely navigating many difficult cultural, social, and religious norms as they were led by the Holy Spirit to establish the early Christian church.

It is quite plausible based on clear scriptural evidence that Paul was also requiring things of women in the few restrictive verses he wrote that God does not require of women.

Every verse of our Bible is inspired. Even if we were to discount the Biblical and historical evidence that certain scriptures were indeed addressing specific issues affecting early church groups, the fact that there is much more Biblical evidence of women operating in and being commended for serving in a variety of leadership positions than there are verses restricting and excluding women from certain positions and expressions should be convincing enough.

It is my belief that the overwhelming Biblical evidence supports equality of men and women in God's eyes and in His callings, gifting's, expressions, abilities etc. Simply put: The Biblical evidence in favor of equality is far more abundant, and the Biblical evidence against equality is much more limited.

Expressions of Women in Ministry

The Pastor and Elder Question

Another helpful point on this issue is that Biblically speaking, all elders are pastors. While all Pastors do not always *vote* as part of an Elder board. It is my belief that *functionally speaking,* Pastors are Elders according to the Bible. With that in mind, the Biblical picture of Pastor and Elder becomes clearer. Peter tells his fellow elders to *shepherd* (Greek: pastor) the flock that is under their care.

5 Now, I encourage you as an elder, an eyewitness of the sufferings of Christ, and one who shares in the glory that is about to be unveiled. I urge my fellow elders among you 2 to be compassionate shepherds who tenderly care for God's flock and who feed them well, for you have the responsibility to guide, protect, and oversee. Consider it a joyous pleasure and not merely a religious duty. Lead from the heart under God's leadership—not as a way to gain finances dishonestly but as a way to eagerly and cheerfully serve. 1 Peter 5:1-2 (TPT)

And Paul told the Ephesian elders to *shepherd* (Greek: pastor) the church of God, which He bought with His own blood. (See Acts 20:17-28).

I have included 2 verses of the scripture from Acts 20:17-28 for reference:

However, from Miletus Paul had sent a message to the elders of the church in Ephesus and asked them to come meet with him. Acts 20:17 (TPT)

At the end of Paul's conversation and visit with the Elders he says:

So guard your hearts. Be true shepherds over all the flock and feed them well. Remember, it was the Holy Spirit who appointed you to guard and oversee the churches that belong to Jesus, the Anointed One, which he purchased and established by his own blood. Acts 20:28 (TPT)

In the previous verses in 1 Peter and Acts there are two other words used for an elder, an *overseer* (or bishop) and *pastor* (or shepherd). Elder, Overseer and Pastor are used synonymously referring to the same position.

As we saw in several New Testament examples, women were clearly pastoring, shepherding, overseeing and caring for Jesus' church.

If according to the Bible a woman can function as a leader, wise councilor, hall of faith member, judge of an entire nation, hero, author of a book in our Bible, queen, preacher, evangelist, official letter carrier for Paul, prophet/prophetess, teacher, pastor / shepherd / overseer, deacon, and apostle, she can most certainly hold any ministry/leadership position in the church today.

The Biblical Pattern Continues

Now that we have looked at the Biblical evidence regarding women in leadership, it is also helpful to see the continuation of God's divine pattern of expressing Himself through both men and women on the earth.

There is an abundance of evidence of God's call to leadership on many women that have greatly impacted the earth for Jesus in our lifetimes as well as in the past. Women that have been called, anointed, and empowered to function in every leadership position in Christ church, thus continuing the divine pattern that

Expressions of Women in Ministry

we saw in the Bible of God using both men and women to express Himself on the earth.

A very small list of these women:

Jarena Lee, Phoebe Palmer, Antoinette Brown Blackwell, Amanda Berry Smith, Maria B. Woodworth-Etter, Aimee Semple McPherson, Kathryn Kuhlman, Mother Teresa, Joan of Arc, Marilyn Hickey, Joyce Meyer, Beth Moore, Paula White, Priscilla Shirer, Bimbo Odukoya, Anna Ziese, Alice Reynolds Flower, Marie Burgess Brown, Elisabeth Elliot

There are also women that I know personally who are amazing leaders in Jesus church, some of these ladies pictures are on the cover of this book. The names of the ladies on the cover are:

Cheryl Easterling, Mary Ann Charles, Kathryn Pacelli, Glory Ingalls, Mary Brook, Autumn Davidson-Zeppa, Julianne Kobelin

Here are a few other scriptures that are relevant to this subject and this document:

13 This "realm of death" describes our former state, for we were held in sin's grasp. But now, we've been resurrected out of that "realm of death" never to return, for we are forever alive and forgiven of all our sins! 14 He canceled out every legal violation we had on our record and the old arrest warrant that stood to indict us. He erased it all—our sins, our stained soul— he deleted it all and they cannot be retrieved! Everything we once were in Adam has been placed onto his cross and nailed permanently there as a public display of cancellation.
Colossians 2:13-14 (TPT)

Therefore if anyone is in Christ [that is, grafted in, joined to Him by faith in Him as Savior], he is a new creature [reborn and renewed by the Holy Spirit]; the old things [the previous moral and spiritual condition] have passed away. Behold, new things have come [because spiritual awakening brings a new life].
2 Corinthians 5:17 (AMP)

Expressions of Women in Ministry

In Christ we are truly set free from sin and its curse! The same curse that has kept us separated from God and each other; the same curse that causes us to elevate or demean according to gender.

28 And we no longer see each other in our former state—Jew or non-Jew, rich or poor, male or female—because we're all one through our union with Jesus Christ with no distinction between us.
Galatians 3:28 (TPT)

The Bible is clear that our loving God *does not show favoritism* (Romans 2:11; 2 Samuel 14:14; 2 Chronicles 19:7; Acts 10:34; Ephesians 6:9). He calls, equips, anoints, empowers, and gives gifts and abilities to whomever He chooses.

As our God does not show favoritism: neither should we.

Closing Thoughts

If a woman is not free to be all God wants her to be, no matter how much limited opportunity she is afforded by male leadership, she will never be fully released to function in any capacity. And as a result, her life as well as the church family that she is part of will not receive the full intended blessings of God through her. If we have limiting mindsets toward women, we not only keep them in bondage, but we also stop God's full expression through them to benefit themselves, their families, the church and the world. In essence, when we limit what God is doing in and through someone, we are quenching the Holy Spirit.

Scriptures that teach this principle of our limitations affecting what we receive are:

Matthew 10:41-42 (NIV) 1 Whoever welcomes a prophet as a prophet will receive a prophet's reward, and whoever welcomes a righteous person as a righteous person will receive a righteous person's reward. 42 And if anyone gives even a cup of cold water to one of these little ones who is my disciple, truly I tell you, that person will certainly not lose their reward."

Matthew 13:57b-58 (TPT) 57b Jesus said, "There's only one place a prophet isn't honored—his own hometown!" 58 And their unbelief kept him from doing many mighty miracles in Nazareth.

Mark 6:4-5(TPT) 4 Jesus said to them, "A prophet is treated with honor everywhere except in his own hometown, among his relatives, and in his own house." 5 He was unable to do any great miracle in

Nazareth, except to heal a few sick people by laying his hands upon them.

The verses we just looked at in Matthew 13:57b-58 and Mark 6:4-5 are applicable to churches that minimize and marginalize their women members/attendees. A limiting and unbelieving mindset regarding women will keep the women from fully embracing and expressing all that God would like to express in and through them, which, in turn will prevent the women from doing mighty works in those churches.

God help every believer, both man and women to:

1 Thessalonians 5:19 (TPT) Never restrain or put out the fire of the Holy Spirit.

An Important Thought for Every Man

Men were created with a unique strength, a God given strength to fight for others, to fight for freedom. Meaning equal freedom for every man, woman and child that Christ died for. Men are not to misuse their strength and fight to keep believers that have been set free by the blood of Jesus captive under the curse.

For the person reading this document, I have a question for you. How much bondage does it take to be in bondage?

Expressions of Women in Ministry

And how much bondage does it take to hinder you from becoming all Christ intends you to be?

On the other hand, how much freedom did Christ die to give us? He died to set both men and women free. Didn't He?

He did not die so either gender could be *almost* free. Did He?

Neither did He die so men could be free and women would remain under the curse.

It was for this freedom that Christ set us free [completely liberating us]; therefore keep standing firm and do not be subject again to a yoke of slavery [which you once removed]. Galatians 5:1(AMP)

So if the Son makes you free, then you are unquestionably free. John 8:36 (AMP)

May God overflow your life with His blessings,

Dana

For more information contact Dana at:

2danaeast@gmail.com

Also, by Dana

"The Prophetic Expression", found on Amazon

Expressions of Women in Ministry

61629722R00046